Science BOOSTER
Book 3

Contents

How do I use this book to boost my performance? ... 2
Check your boost ... 4

AT2 Living things
Eating words ★ ... 6
Good food ★ ... 7
Kinds of teeth ★★ ... 8
Look after your teeth ★ ... 9
What do cats eat? ★★ ... 10
Who eats more fruit? ★★ ... 11
Who eats the most fruit? ★★ ... 12
Growing words ★★ ... 13
How does your garden grow? ★ ... 14
Animal or plant? ★★ ... 15
Parts of a plant ★ ... 16
Are plants alive? ★★ ... 17
How much water do plants need? ★★ ... 18
Understanding bar charts ★★ ... 19

AT3 Materials
It's a material world ★ ... 20
What is everything made of? ★ ... 21
What is it like? ★★ ... 22
Why is it made from that? ★ ... 23
What should we choose? ★★ ... 24

Testing towels ★★ ... 25
Making sense of results ★★ ... 26
Spell it right ★ ... 27
Rocks and soils ★ ... 28
Rocks and their uses ★ ... 29
Where do you find rocks? ★★ ... 30
Soils ★ ... 31
Rocky tests ★★ ... 32
Explaining results ★★ ... 33

AT4 Physical processes
New words ★★ ... 34
Magnets – the key facts ★ ... 35
Magnetic and non-magnetic ★★ ... 36
Springs ★ ... 37
Uses of magnets and springs ★★ ... 38
Testing magnets ★★ ... 39
Comparing magnets ★★ ... 40
Light wordpower ★ ... 41
Shadows ★ ... 42
The Sun's shadows ★★ ... 43
Daytime shadows ★ ... 44
Predicting ★★ ... 45
Are the predictions any good? ★★ ... 46

Glossary ... 47

How do I use this book to boost my performance?

Each unit in this book is set out in the same way. Each one will help boost your understanding of science and become better at investigations.

The questions and activities in each unit can be done as part of normal classwork, or for homework in the form of a booster lesson.

Each of the units should fit in with the work you are doing in Year 3.

To help you get the best out of the book:

- read each unit slowly and carefully. Give yourself time to think about the ideas.
- work closely with your teacher or friends so that you share each other's ideas.
- do all of the activities in the order they have been set out. This will help you feel the boost.
- go back to any units you find difficult a few days later, after the ideas have had time to sink in.
- if you don't understand what something means, ask someone who can help you with it.

Key idea
Don't ignore this key idea. It tells you the most important idea in the unit.

Each unit has a star rating
★ A one-star unit has been written to ensure you are working at Level 3.
★★ A two-star unit has been written to help boost your performance to a higher level.

Warm up
This task should take around five to ten minutes. It will help you and your teacher to get your brain working and to start to identify how much you need boosting.

Lift off
This activity will take you about ten to 20 minutes to complete. In a one-star unit it often revisits an idea you have come across before. In a two-star unit it helps you think about an idea you have recently learned.

The booster
This activity will also take around ten to 20 minutes to complete. It is harder than the 'Lift off' activity and, if you do it well, it will help to boost your understanding or skills to a higher level.

Testing magnets ★★

Tests need to be done fairly

Warm up

Will is thinking about what affects how strong a magnet is. His idea is that: 'long magnets are stronger than short ones'.

Which of these might also affect how strong a magnet is?

- The colour it is painted.
- How heavy it is.
- The surface it is on.
- The metal it is made from.
- Its shape.
- The direction it points.

Lift off

Will has come up with a way of testing his idea. However, his plan is in the wrong order.

A Add paperclips one by one.

B Then do the test on each of the other magnets in turn.

C Keep on adding the paperclips until no more can be added.

D Record how many paperclips could be added to each magnet.

E Get some paperclips and some magnets of different sizes.

F Take the smallest magnet.

Redraw his plan in order.

The booster

Will's plan is not yet complete. Some details are missing.

1. How could Will make sure his test was fair?
2. How many measurements should he take?
3. How should he record his measurements?
4. Now write out his complete plan in the best order.

Checkpoint

There are some other ideas you could test. Write down some other things that might make magnets stronger.

For example, you could test the idea that: 'horseshoe magnets are stronger than bar magnets'.

Checkpoint
Most of these activities take about five to ten minutes to complete, although some are a little longer. If you do this well, it means the boost has worked.

Top tips
These contain important information and tips to help you complete the activities.

Check your boost

What to do

Make a copy of these two pages. Before you start your work, assess how well you think you can tackle each task.

Tick ☹ if you cannot do the task at all.

Tick 😐 if you can do some of the task.

Tick ☺ if you can already do the task well.

Focus on areas where you are weak first. As you complete each unit, try to convert a ☹ to a ☺. Mark it on your sheet. Keep a progress check on how many areas you have boosted.

Can you:	☹	😐	☺
name a lot of words to do with eating?			
choose food that keeps you healthy?			
spot different kinds of teeth?			
explain how to look after your teeth?			
explain why cats have the teeth they do?			
decide how many times you need to repeat a fair test?			
use results to draw a conclusion?			
use words to do with growing?			
describe some places that suit plants?			
describe the uses of some common plants?			
name the parts of a plant and what they do?			
tell how something is alive?			

Can you:	☹	😐	🙂
plan how to test to see how much water a plant needs?			
make sense of the data in a bar chart?			
explain why some materials suit the jobs they do?			
describe what some common things are made of?			
describe what some materials look and feel like?			
choose a good material for some everyday objects?			
explain why some materials are better for some things than others?			
plan how to test paper towels to decide which one is best?			
work out the meaning of test results?			
spell some words to do with rocks and soils correctly?			
explain how soils are formed?			
name some useful properties of rocks?			
describe the places where rocks are found?			
spot the differences between two kinds of soil?			
plan a test to see how fast water flows through different rocks?			
make sense of the observations in a fair test?			
use scientific words that describe magnets?			
remember some key facts about magnets?			
tell the difference between a magnetic and a non-magnetic material?			
describe what happens to springs when they are stretched?			
say how magnets and springs are used in everyday life?			
test the strength of magnets?			
explain what the results of some tests on magnets mean?			
use some words to describe light?			
explain how a shadow is formed?			
explain how the Sun appears to move across the sky?			
describe how shadows change through the day?			
predict the kinds of shadows formed by opaque, transparent and translucent materials?			
decide if the evidence from a test supports a prediction?			
use a glossary to help you understand the scientific words you use?			

Eating words

Words have special meanings in science

Warm up How many words can you think of to do with eating?
Go around your class and see how many you can find. Make a list.

Lift off Copy the table. Match up each word in the box with its meaning.

activity   grinding   feeding   growth

Word	Meaning
	Getting larger
	Taking in food
	Breaking something up into tiny pieces
	Movements like running and jumping

The booster Our teeth have tricky names. It can help you to remember them if you know some word tricks.

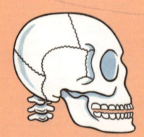

INCISORS Like the word **SCISSORS**. **Scissors** cut cloth; **incisors** cut food.

CANINES Canine means **DOG**.

MOLARS A **MILLER** grinds up wheat to make flour; **molars** grind food.

Why do you think canine teeth are named after the word for 'dog'? Write your explanation: 'I think canine teeth are named after the word 'dog' because …'

Checkpoint Put your 'Warm up' list of eating words into: 'Words to do with teeth', 'Words to do with chewing' and 'Words to do with food'.

Words to do with teeth
Incisor, canine, molar, grinding, cutting, biting

Good food

You need to eat different kinds of food to stay healthy

Warm up What is your favourite meal? There are so many nice things to choose from!

Ask your friends which meal they like the most. Draw up a table to show what they like.

Lift off There are lots of different types of food. **Roast beef** is a type of **meat**.

Copy the table. Put each food shown above in the correct column to show what type of food it is. One has been done for you.

Type of food	First example	Second example
Meat and fish	Roast beef	
Fats and oils		
Starches and sugars		
Vegetables		
Fruit		

The booster Different types of food have different jobs. That's why you need to eat lots of different food every day. You use some food to run and jump – it helps you be **active**. Other food builds up your body – you use it to **grow**.

Pick some food for activity and some for growth. Put them in a table.

Food for activity	Food for growth

Checkpoint Fruit and vegetables are very good for you. Write down the names of all the fruit and vegetables you ate today.

You should try to eat at least five portions of fruit and vegetables a day to keep healthy!

Kinds of teeth

Different teeth have different jobs

Warm up Have you ever noticed that not all your teeth are the same shape?

Use a safety mirror or magnifying lens to look at your teeth. How many different shapes can you see?

Lift off You have different kinds of teeth.

Match up the name of each tooth with the correct description.

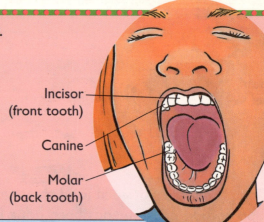

incisor   canine   molar

Description	Type of tooth
Wide 'double' teeth with flat tops	
Long pointed teeth	
Sharp, flat, cutting teeth	

The booster Patrick explained how the shape of the canines helps them to do their job.

Make up two more sentences like Patrick's.

Explain why the incisors and the molars are the right shape for their jobs.

Canines can hold and tear food into smaller pieces because they are pointed.

Checkpoint Now let's see if you have understood all of this!

1 Which teeth do you use to bite off a piece of apple?
2 Which teeth do you use to chew up some meat?
3 Which teeth do you use to hold and tear food?

Look after your teeth

If you look after your teeth, they will last

Warm up

You have probably lost some of your first (milk) teeth. Your next ones will have to last you a lifetime.

Find out how many of the grown-ups you know have still got all their teeth. Ask nicely!

Lift off

Some food helps keep your teeth healthy. Other food can harm them.

Toffee is bad for your teeth. It sticks to them. The sugar in it makes teeth go bad. Celery is good for your teeth. There is no sugar in it and it cleans your teeth.

Put these food and drinks into the right column in a table like this.

celery   toffee   jam   apples
chocolate   lemonade   milk   tomatoes

Bad for your teeth	Good for your teeth
toffee	celery

The booster

You need to brush your teeth at least twice a day to make them last.

Explain why you need to brush your teeth. Write out these sentences in order.

A Brushing your teeth gets rid of the sugar.

B Sugar turns to acid in your mouth.

C Acid attacks your teeth.

D Clean teeth will last much longer.

E Food on your teeth for a long time causes more damage.

F Sticky food clings to your teeth.

Checkpoint

Lots of people have a milky drink and a biscuit before they go to bed.

Explain why you should always clean your teeth *after* your bedtime snack.

What do cats eat?

Cats have special teeth to help when they hunt

Warm up

Do all animals eat the same food?

Does anyone in your class know what these animals eat?

- dogs   horses   ducks
- cows   thrushes frogs

Lift off

Pet cats don't usually eat vegetables or fruit – they like meat. Tinned cat food contains a lot of meat.

1. List all the things you know cats eat. Ask your friends to help you find out more.

   > Things cats eat:
   > Mice
   > Tinned cat food

   Think about what a pet cat could catch. It can't be very big!

2. What do you think wild cats, like lions, usually eat?

The booster

Pet cats are hunters, just like tigers and lions. They need special teeth to help them.

Pick the right reason why cats have such long canine teeth.

- To chew their meat well.
- To pick up leaves to eat.
- To bite and kill mice.
- To clean their fur.

Incisor (front tooth)
Canine
Molar (back tooth)

Checkpoint

Now think about your own teeth.

Why do you think humans have quite small canine teeth?

Who eats more fruit?

> Make sure you do a test enough times

Warm up

A banana is a fruit. A cabbage is a vegetable. But what about a tomato – is it a fruit or a vegetable? What *is* a fruit?

List all the fruit you can think of.

Lift off

Celia noticed something interesting at lunchtime. Aidan did not agree.

"Boys don't eat as much fruit as girls."

"I bet we do. Let's find out for sure."

Is Celia right? Do girls eat more fruit than boys?

1. Which is the best question to ask the boys and girls?
   - Do you like fruit?
   - Did you eat any fruit today?

2. What would be a good number of people to ask?
   - Two – just Celia and Aidan.
   - Just the ones on their table.
   - As many people as possible.

The booster

There were ten girls that Celia could ask about eating fruit, but the only boy was Aidan.

"That's not really fair. What if the other boys eat more fruit than I do?"

"You are right. What should I do now?"

How could Celia make her test fairer?

Checkpoint

Do you think there might be any other differences between what boys and girls eat? Try some tests like Celia's to find out.

Who eats the most fruit?

You need to think about what results mean

Warm up — Check with your teacher what the word 'conclusion' means.

Lift off — Celia and Aidan asked their friends about eating fruit.

Here are their results:

Girl's names	Eaten fruit today?
Celia	Yes
Judi	Yes
Angela	No
Lucy	Yes
Irene	No
Kamlesh	Yes
Patrice	Yes
Sharon	Yes
Mina	Yes
Poppy	No

Boy's names	Eaten fruit today?
Aidan	No
Dominic	Yes
Daniel	No
Billy	No
Shazad	Yes
Finton	No
John	Yes
Mohammed	No
Parminder	No
Rene	No

Have you eaten any fruit today?

Yes.

Count the 'Yes' answers and the 'No' answers. Put the totals in a table like this.

	YES – Ate some fruit	NO – Did not eat any fruit
Girls		
Boys		

The booster — Now you need to think about what the results really mean. Pick the correct conclusion:

- Boys eat more fruit than girls.
- Girls eat more fruit than boys.
- Boys and girls eat the same amount of fruit.

Was I right when I said girls eat more fruit than boys?

Checkpoint — Now you know what the answer was in Celia's class. What do you think it would be in yours? Try it out!

Growing words

Plants need light, warmth and water to grow

Warm up — How many different words do you know that help describe a plant?

Lift off — Mrs Sharma has two apple trees in her garden. One is healthy but the other one is very sick.

Copy and complete the table. Write each word from the box in the best place in your table.

slowly   sour   thin   weak   yellow

	Healthy tree	Unhealthy tree
The leaves will be …	green	
The trunk will be …	thick	
The roots will be …	strong	
The fruit will be …	sweet	
The whole tree grows …	quickly	

The booster — The word 'because' links a fact to the reason for it. For example: 'Not many plants grow in the desert *because* there is not enough water.'

Link up each fact to the right reason.

Facts

- Not much grows at the South Pole because …
- Grass dies under a brick because …
- A cactus can live in the desert because …

Reasons

- … it is too cold for plants to grow there.
- … it can store water.
- … plants need light to grow.

Checkpoint — Write one sentence to say what plants need to grow properly.

How does your garden grow?

Plants grow in places that suit them

Warm up Do you do any gardening? Do any of your friends or family? Does anyone in your class know how to make a garden grow well? Draw some pictures of your ideas.

Lift off Each of these pictures shows Mary making sure her plants are getting something they need.

Pick three words from the box to say what plants need to grow properly.

> sunlight   wind   water   shade   snow   warmth

The booster There are some places where plants struggle to grow. This is because something they need is not there.

Look at these places where not much will grow. Say what is missing in each one.

Place	What is it like?	What is missing?
A desert	Hot and sunny	
Under a tree	Warm and wet	
The South Pole	Sunny and wet	

Checkpoint Now go back to your pictures of ideas from the 'Warm up'.

Write a sentence or two to explain why different plants grow in places that suit them.

Animal or plant?

Plants are grown for food and other uses

Warm up

How many different kinds of food can you think of that are made from plants?

Make a list by asking around the class.

Your teacher will write the list on the board to help you.

Lift off

Apples grow on trees and milk comes from cows. Sand is just there in the ground – it's not from a plant or an animal.

Where do these useful things come from? Copy the table and put them in the right column.

> apples   leather   iron   clay
> wood   meat   sand   milk   cotton

From a plant	From an animal	From the ground

The booster

Now think about plants. Some are for food. Some are used for other things.

Write some sentences about the things that plants are used for. The first one has been done for you.

For food	Lettuces, tomatoes and apples all come from plants.
For clothes	
For furniture	
For decoration (to look nice)	

Checkpoint

Find out more about how bread is made. Think about:
- the plant it is made from.
- the part of the plant that is used.
- how flour is made.
- how the baker turns flour into bread.

Parts of a plant

Different parts of a plant do different jobs

Warm up

We eat the roots, stems and leaves of many plants. Copy and complete the table. Fill in each column with the names of some of these plants.

We eat the root	We eat the stem	We eat the leaves
Carrots		

Lift off

There are many different parts to a plant. Copy the table. Match up each part to the correct label letter in the picture.

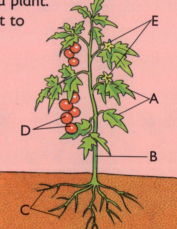

Part of the plant	Letter
Leaves	
Roots	
Stem	
Flower	
Fruit	

The booster

Different parts of a plant do different jobs.

1 Copy the table. Match up each part of the plant with the job it does.

leaves   stem   roots

Part of the plant	The job it does
	Carries water from the roots to the leaves
	Soaks up water from the ground
	Collects sunlight to help make food

2 Write down one other job that the roots do.

Checkpoint

Explain why a plant would die if you cut off its leaves.

Think about how the leaves help a plant to live. What couldn't it do if the leaves were not there?

Are plants alive?

Plants are alive because they grow and make new plants

Warm up Look around your classroom and out of the window. You will see many plants and many things made from plants.

Make two lists, like this:

Plants	Things made from plants
grass	paper

Lift off Look at the family in this picture. They are using lots of plants.

List all the things this family use plants for. For example: 'They will eat the bananas.'

The booster Plants are living things. They all die some day. Dead flowers dry up and fall to the ground. Dead trees fall down and new ones are planted.

Which of these things show us that an oak tree is alive?

- It grows bigger every year.
- It produces new leaves each summer.
- It has branches.
- It is made of wood.
- The acorns grow into new trees.
- It is very tall.

A little acorn will grow into a big tree

Checkpoint Now see if you can tell the difference between something that is alive and something that is not. Complete this sentence: 'You can tell a brick is not alive because ...'

How much water do plants need? ⭐⭐

Make sure some things are kept the same in a fair test

Warm up

Do you help in the garden? What makes plants grow well?

Write a list of all the things you can do to look after plants.

Lift off

How much water should you give to bean seedlings? Stephen thought that more water would make them grow better.

Here are the things he did. Draw the pictures again in order.

A Write down the results.

B Give each seedling a different amount of water.

C Measure the height of each seedling.

D Pick six seedlings the same size.

The booster

Meera asked Stephen why he was so fussy when picking his seedlings.

Why do you want them all the same size?

Well, I have to do that because …

How will Stephen explain why he wanted all his seedlings the same size at the start of the test?

Checkpoint

What else did Stephen need to keep the same every time? Choose two from these:

- The temperature
- Who waters the plants
- Who writes the results
- The amount of light.

Understanding bar charts ★★

Bar charts can help you to understand results

Warm up
Ask your friends to tell you the colour of your headteacher's car. Do they all agree? How would you find out the right answer?

Lift off
All of Stephen's seedlings were 5cm tall to start with. He measured how tall the plants were one week later. He drew a bar chart of his results.

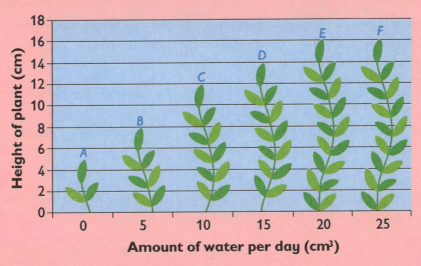

1. One plant had not grown at all. How much water had it been given?
2. How tall was the plant which had been given 15cm³ of water each day?
3. Which plants grew the most? How tall were they?

The booster
Now decide what the results mean.

Pick the right conclusion for Stephen's test.

- It doesn't make any difference how much water you give a plant.
- The more water you give a plant, the more it grows
- The less water you give a plant, the better it grows.

Checkpoint
The results for 20cm³ and 25cm³ of water were the same. That might mean two things. *Either* Stephen measured one plant wrongly *or* 20cm³ of water is enough for the plant so it is not worth giving it any more.

How could you decide which reason is correct? Write down your answer.

It's a material world

There is a material suitable for every job

Warm up

Brick is a material used to build part of a house. **Wood** can be used to make tables.

How many materials can you think of? Make a big list and share it with your friends.

Material doesn't just mean **cloth**. A material is something that can be used to make something else.

Lift off

Here are some words to learn. They tell us what materials are like.

Copy the sentences and fill in each gap with the correct word.

> strong   transparent   flexible   absorbent   hard

a A brick is _____, which means it can take a lot of weight.

b Concrete is _____, which means it won't wear out when you walk on it.

c A plastic ruler is _____, which means it is bendy.

d A towel is _____, which means it soaks up water.

e Glass is _____, which means you can see through it.

The booster

You can use the words in the 'Lift off' to compare different materials. For example, you could say that brick is stronger than paper.

Think of a material that you could use to finish each sentence.

a Brick is **stronger** than _____.

b Concrete is **harder** than _____.

c A plastic ruler is more **flexible** than _____.

d A towel is more **absorbent** than _____.

e Glass is more **transparent** than _____.

This path should be harder!

Checkpoint

Look back at the list of materials you made in the 'Warm up'. Find a good word to describe each one.

brick – hard

What is everything made of?

Many different materials are used to make things

Warm up Paper and cardboard are very useful. Many different things are made from them.

List all the uses of paper or cardboard in your home.

Lift off A material is anything you can make something else with. Plastic can be used to make toys, for example.

Look at this supermarket.
List all the materials you can see.

In the picture I can see things made of:
leather

The booster Each material is being used for more than one thing. For example, one woman in the supermarket has shoes made of leather and a leather handbag.

Write two uses for the other materials you can spot in the supermarket. Put them in a table, like this.

Material	First use	Second use
leather	shoes	handbag

Checkpoint Do you know what your shoes are made of? It could be more than one thing. How about your socks? Do any of your clothes have buttons? Clothes are made from so many different things!

List all the different materials your clothes can be made from.

What is it like?

Some words describe what a material is like

Warm up

How many words can you think of to describe a car?

Go around your class and see how many words you can list.

Lift off

Here are some words that are used to describe materials.

soft   yellow   slippery   shiny   thick   absorbent

Choose the correct words to fill in the gaps below. For example: 'Glass is transparent and hard.'

a Gold is _____ and _____.

b Oil is _____ and _____.

c Cloth is _____ and _____.

The booster

Now you know about describing materials, it is time to play a game.

Think of a material and describe it to your friend. Say what it is used for and what it is like. Your friend has to guess what it is.

Checkpoint

Metal and ice are both smooth and shiny. These are two ways they are the **same**. Can you think of one way they are **different**?

Why is it made from that?

You need to choose the right material for every job

Warm up

Would clothes made out of paper be any good? Could you have a house made out of plastic?

Say what would be wrong with these ideas.

- a paper coat
- a car made of clay
- a plastic house
- a metal hat
- a wooden window
- a chocolate teapot

Lift off

Here are some different materials.

concrete   plastic   rubber   gold   china   wool

Which one would you pick to make these things?

A ring for your finger		Garden chairs	
A path in a garden		Tyres for a car	
A winter scarf		A teacup	

The booster

Why is glass used to make windows? Because it lets light in, of course! A window that you couldn't see through wouldn't be much good.

Complete these sentences. Choose the correct word to explain why each material is used.

waterproof   strong   transparent   absorbent   soft

a Glass is _____ so it lets plenty of light through a window.

b Paper is _____ so a tissue soaks up plenty of water.

c Bricks are _____ so they are good for building a house.

d Cotton is _____ so clothes feel comfortable.

e Plastic is _____ so it stops things getting wet.

Checkpoint

Now go back to your 'Lift off' answers. Explain why you chose each one. For example, 'I chose wool for a winter scarf *because* it would keep my neck warm.'

What should we choose? ⭐⭐

Some materials are better than others at their job

Warm up
Trainers should be light, not heavy. What else should trainers be like? List some ideas.

Lift off
Sometimes, two materials can be chosen to make something.

Try these ideas:
It does not **break** easily.
It does not **melt** easily.
It does not **tear** easily.

Explain why one material is better than the other in each of these examples.

a A table needs to be **hard**.
   Wood and glass are both hard.
   Why is wood the best material to make a table?

   Wood is best for a table **because** …

b A T-shirt needs to be **soft**.
   Cotton and paper are both soft.
   Why is cotton the best material to make a T-shirt?

   Cotton is best for a T-shirt **because** …

c A saucepan needs to be **waterproof**.
   Iron and plastic are both waterproof.
   Why is iron the best material for a saucepan?

   Iron is best for a saucepan **because** …

The booster
Can you think of different materials to do some other jobs?

Pick a different, but suitable, material for each of these jobs.

a A window is normally made from glass but it could be made from _____.
b A towel is normally made from cloth but it could be made from _____.
c A ring is normally made from gold but it could be made from _____.
d A plate can be made from plastic or _____.

Checkpoint
Toy trains used to be made out of metal. Now they are made from plastic.

Write down why you think plastic is better than metal for a toy train.

Testing towels ⭐⭐

Some things are kept the same in fair tests

Warm up What makes a good paper towel? Here is an idea to start you off: 'A good paper towel will soak up a lot of water'.

Make a list of some more good ideas.

Lift off Sally wanted to know which paper towel soaked up the most water. She tested some by seeing how many drops of water each one would soak up.

Here are the things she did. Draw them again in order.

A Write down the results.

B Do it again with the other paper towels.

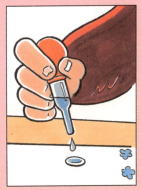

C Count how many drops the towel can soak up.

D Lay one of the paper towels on the table.

The booster Ben spotted that the test wasn't fair.

That's not fair. One of your towels was bigger than the others.

You're right. I can put that right. I will …

1 What will Sally say to Ben about how she can improve her test?

2 Ben also noticed that one of the towels was given much bigger drops of water. How will Sally put that right?

Checkpoint Now list the things (factors) in her test that Sally should keep the same every time.

Making sense of results

Sometimes two people's results don't agree

Warm up

Ask your friends what colour the curtains are in the school hall. Do they all say the same thing? If not, how would you find out the right answer?

Lift off

Sally put the results of her paper towel test in a bar chart.

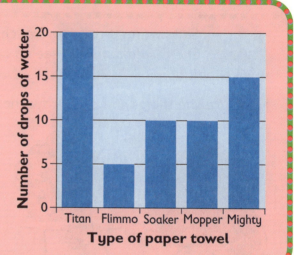

1. Which towel only soaked up five drops of water?
2. Which two towels both soaked up the same amount of water?
3. Which would be the best towel to buy?
4. Which is the worst?

The booster

Just to check, Ben tried the test. Here are his results.

Type of paper towel	Number of drops of water it soaked up
Titan	18
Flimmo	7
Soaker	12
Mopper	6
Mighty	14

My results are similar to Sally's but there are some differences.

1. Make a bar chart like Sally's using Ben's results.
2. Ben's results are not the same as Sally's. Why do you think that is?
3. Which paper towel would Ben say was the best?
4. Which would he say was the worst?

Checkpoint

Ben and Sally did not agree about which paper towel was the worst. What should they do now?

Spell it right

Be careful when spelling new words

Warm up

How many types of rocks and soils do you know?

List as many rocks and soils as you can in one minute.

Now share your list with a friend. Make a longer list. Make sure each rock and soil is spelled correctly.

Lift off

Sam finds spelling hard. Here is his list of some rocks and soils.

Spot the spelling mistake in each word. Write each one out correctly.

Slaet	Marbel
Grannite	Chalke
Cley	Sande

The booster

Now let's see if you can spot some misspelled words. Rewrite this paragraph correctly. Correct all the spelling mistakes.

Rocs were made a lonng time ago. There are many differrent kindes of roc. Chalke is a sofft, whit roc. It is very crumbely. It was formed from milleons of shells of tini sea creattures which dyed a long time ago. As they ley on the botom of the sea, there weight crushed them together to form the roc. Grannite is another roc. It was once a reed hot liqud which came from beneef the Earth's surfase. This slowly cooled down. When it was colde, it turrned into a harde, shiney roc.

Checkpoint

Let's see how much you have learned!

Make a poster of rock and soil words showing some common spelling mistakes.

Make your poster eye catching. Show the correct spellings as well as the common mistakes.

Rocks and soils

Soils are ground down rocks

Warm up
Discuss the differences between a rock, a stone, a pebble and a soil.

Lift off
Rocks are one type of material that is found in nature. Other materials are manufactured (made by humans).

1. Sort these materials into those that are found in nature and those that are not.

- iron
- sandstone
- gold
- wood
- limestone
- shampoo
- plastic
- slate

2. Now sort them into rocks and other materials.
3. Can you sort them in any other ways?

The booster
Soils are made from broken down rocks and other materials.

Lauren mixed some soil and water together.

Key
Water
Chalk
Clay
Sand
Gravel

1. Where are the biggest particles found when the soil settles?
2. Where are the smallest particles found when the soil settles?
3. Can you say anything about the size of the particles and where they settle?

Checkpoint
Now see if you can explain why soils in water settle out in the way that they do.

Rocks and their uses

Many rocks have useful properties

Warm up Which of these words might describe a rock?

smelly   hard   soapy   multicoloured   shiny   soft
gassy   hot   attractive   magnetic   opaque   clear

Lift off Different rocks look and feel different.

1 Look carefully at these four rocks. Copy the table and fill in the 'What it looks like' column.

2 Then use some real rocks or library books to fill in the other two columns.

Name of rock	What it looks like	What it feels like	Other features
Granite			
Sandstone			
Slate			
Limestone			

Granite

Sandstone

Slate

Limestone

The booster Rocks are used for certain jobs because of their properties. For example, granite is used to make steps in buildings because it does not wear away easily.

Use sentences with 'because' in them to explain why:

a Sandstone is used to build the walls of churches *because* …
b Slate is used for roofs *because* …
c Limestone is used to build walls in a farmers field *because* …

Checkpoint Now let's how much you have learned.

What features would be useful if a rock were to be used for the following:

a a pavement stone   b a photograph frame   c a blackboard   d a monument?

Where do you find rocks? ⭐⭐

> Rocks are found beneath the Earth's surface

Warm up Discuss with your friends where they have found rocks before. Write a few sentences about what they say. Draw some pictures if these will help.

Lift off There are rocks on and under the Earth's surface. Look closely and you will find them.

I know granite and marble. But there are lots more.

1 List all the places you can see rocks in the picture.
2 Write down the names of as many rocks as you can.

The booster Some rocks are hard to see. They might be hidden by buildings or soil.

1 Draw a detailed plan of your school.
2 Go outside with your friends. Add as many types of rocks to your plan as you can.

Checkpoint Now do some more research into rocks.

1 Surf the Internet and look for pictures of some interesting rocks. Start with the following:

| The Grand Canyon | Tabletop mountain | Ayers rock | Mount Everest |

2 Make an interesting poster of your findings.

Soils ⭐

Soils are mostly made from small pieces of rock

Warm up — Make an interesting collection of rocks and soils for your classroom. Write labels to describe each rock in your collection.

Lift off — Soils are made when rocks are ground down.

Which things in the picture help to wear down rocks to make soil?

The booster — Different soils contain different amounts of ground down rocks.

Mark shook up two different soils in water. He let them settle. This is what he saw.

Tip: Measure the height of each part of each soil. Use your ruler accurately.

Key:
- Chalk
- Clay
- Sand
- Gravel

1. Which soil contains the most chalk?
2. Which soil contains the most clay?
3. Which soil has the same amount (volume) of clay and gravel?
4. Does Soil A contain two, three or four times the amount of sand than Soil B?

Checkpoint — As well as very small pieces of rock, soil can contain other things. Use your school library books to find out some other things than are found in soil.

Rocky tests

Tests need to be done fairly

Warm up Jade wanted to find out how easily water flowed through different kinds of soils. What equipment in this selection would she NOT need?

Lift off Here are her first ideas on how to do the test. Look carefully at what she did.

Put different soils into the containers.

Add water and leave.

See what happens to the water.

Jade kept getting different results each time. She didn't carry out a fair test.

1. How much soil should she have put into the two containers at the start?
2. Should this soil have been dry or wet?
3. What is wrong with the amounts of water she added to each container? How much water should she have added?
4. What else should she do instead of just looking at what happens to the water?

The booster Scientific tests need to be fair. If they are, you will have a result you can trust.

Redraw Jade's diagrams showing how she could make her test fair.

Checkpoint Now let's check if you made the test fair. Copy and complete this table to show the things (factors) you kept the same, those you changed and those you measured to make this a fair test.

What I kept the same	What I changed	What I measured

Explaining results

The results of scientific tests need to be explained

Warm up

Jade tested how quickly water passed though clay soil, sandy soil and loamy soil. She made some predictions.

- Water will pass equally quickly through each soil.
- Water will pass most quickly through the soil with the smallest particles.
- Water will pass most quickly through the soil with the largest particles.

Which of her predictions do you think is the best? Explain why.

Lift off

Jade tried her test four times. She put her test results in a table. Look at the information carefully. It shows the volume of water that went through each soil in 30 minutes.

1. What do the results show about how quickly water flows through different soils?
2. Explain why the results for one soil are not all the same.

	Clay soil	Loamy soil	Sandy soil
1st test	20cm^3	35cm^3	45cm^3
2nd test	19cm^3	33cm^3	45cm^3
3rd test	20cm^3	37cm^3	42cm^3
4th test	21cm^3	35cm^3	45cm^3

The booster

These diagrams show the kinds of particles in each of the different soils. Look at them carefully.

clay soil

sandy soil

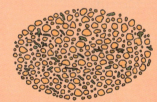
loamy soil

1. Which soils contain just one size of particle?
2. Which soil is a mixture of different-sized particles?
3. Which soil has: **a** the biggest particles **b** the smallest particles?

Checkpoint

Now you should be able to explain how soils are made.

Explain the results of Jade's test using your knowledge of what soils are made of.

New words

Some words describe magnets well

Warm up

All these words are to do with magnets but the letters have been mixed up.

Unjumble each word to reveal the mystery word.

TRATACT   PEREL   ROCEF   SOLEP   ROHOHSESE

This one is difficult so here's a clue! It's curved and said to bring good luck.

Lift off

1 What does each mystery word mean? Join up each word with its meaning.

Word

- TRATACT
- PEREL
- ROCEF
- ROHOHSESE
- SOLEP

Meaning

- A curved magnet
- A push or pull
- Push away
- The ends of a magnet
- Pull towards

2 Write a sentence using each mystery word to show that you understand its meaning.

The booster

Now let's see if you can use each word correctly. Use each unjumbled word once to complete these sentences.

a Each magnet has two _____, where their effect is concentrated.

b Bar magnets and _____ magnets are the two most common magnet shapes.

c Two magnets can either _____ or _____ each other.

d The magnetic _____ can be felt all around a magnet.

Checkpoint

Now let's see how much you have learned!

Draw some diagrams of different magnets. Use the words you have just learned to label them.

Magnets – the key facts

Magnets can attract or repel each other

Warm up

Magnets come in different shapes and sizes.

Which magnet in the picture is the:

a bar
b circular
c horseshoe
d wand
e ceramic magnet?

Lift off

Magnets are usually made from iron. Two magnets attract (pull towards) or repel (push away) each other. **Like** poles **repel** and **unlike** poles **attract**.

a 🟥🟦 🟥🟦   b 🟥🟦 🟦🟥

1 Which pair of magnets will attract each other?
2 Which pair of magnets will repel each other?
3 Draw another way in which two magnets will repel each other.
4 Draw two horseshoe magnets attracted to each other.

Red indicates the north pole of a magnet. Blue indicates the south pole.

The booster

Some magnets are stronger than others. Will tested this. He drew a pictogram of how many steel paperclips different magnets could pick up. Look at his results.

Large bar magnet	📎📎📎📎📎
Small bar magnet	📎📎📎
Large horseshoe magnet	📎📎
Small horseshoe magnet	📎📎📎📎

Which of these are true or false?

- The small horseshoe magnet was the weakest.
- The large bar magnet picked up seven paperclips.
- Large magnets are always stronger than small ones.
- The small horseshoe magnet is twice as strong as the large horseshoe magnet.

Checkpoint

Now do a test of your own to see if magnets work through other materials, such as card, fabric, aluminium foil and paper. Make table to show your results.

Magnetic and non-magnetic

Magnets and magnetic materials are two different things

Warm up
Which of the following metals are attracted to a magnet?

iron   gold   aluminium   lead   tin   steel

Lift off
Magnetic materials are attracted by a magnet. Magnets only attract a very few metals. Iron or steel are the ones you need to spot at this stage. Other materials are non-magnetic. This means magnets have no effect on them.

1 Copy the table. Tick (✓) the materials that are attracted to a magnet. Put a cross (✗) against those that are not.

Material/Object	Magnetic (✓ or ✗)	Material/Object	Magnetic (✓ or ✗)
Gold ring		Wooden pencil	
Aluminium foil		Iron nail	
Plastic spoon		Copper bracelet	
Steel knife		Silver medal	
Steel paperclip		Paper cup	

2 List some more materials that are non-magnetic.

The booster
Magnets help you test if a material is magnetic or not.

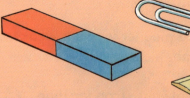

1 What would happen if each of these objects were brought close to a magnet?

2 Explain in your own words how you would tell if something was magnetic or non-magnetic.

*Two magnets always attract or repel each other. A magnetic material is **always** attracted to a magnet, never repelled. Magnets have no effect on non-magnetic materials.*

Checkpoint
Besides iron and some steels, there are only two other metals that are magnetic and can be made into a magnet. Find out which two metals these are.

Springs ⭐

Forces help springs stretch

Warm up
Springs change shape when you pull them apart or push them together.

Draw what happens when you push or pull a spring like this one shown.

Lift off
Look carefully at this spring stretching.

Which of these statements are true? Which are false? Make a table to show this.

- The spring gets heavier as you pull it.
- A force is needed to pull the spring apart.
- If you let the stretched spring go, nothing will happen.
- Another word for 'stretch' is 'extend'.
- The more you pull a spring, it the shorter it gets.
- Springs are usually made from metal.

True	False

The booster
In what direction do forces act? Describe in your own words the direction of the two forces in each of these diagrams.

a

b

Checkpoint
Let's see how well you can describe a spring stretching. Write a poem or an exciting description of a spring stretching. Make sure you use all the words in the box. Use some of your own words as well.

> force   expand   size   pull   stretch   shape

Uses of magnets and springs ⭐⭐

Magnets and springs have many uses

Warm up

Magnets are used around the home. They can be very useful.

List the ways in which magnets are used in everyday life.

Amazingly, magnets are used in loudspeakers. They help to turn an electrical signal into the sound you hear.

Lift off

Magnets are useful because they attract each other and other magnetic metals.

Decide if the following are True or False.

When magnets are used to hold two things together, the two items are made from:	True	False
two magnetic metals		
one magnet and one magnetic metal		
one magnet and one non-magnetic metal		
two magnets with their like poles together		
two magnets with their unlike poles together		

The booster

Springs are also useful. They can help to push things apart.

1. Explain how the springs in a stapler and a pen help them to work.
2. Draw cut-away pictures of a mattress and an armchair. Show how the springs help to make them comfortable.

Checkpoint

Now let's add more uses for springs to your 'Warm up' list.

Find out how springs are used in cars or bicycles to make their ride more comfortable. Then find out how magnets are used to recycle used cans.

You could use the Internet or books in your school library to do this.

Testing magnets

Tests need to be done fairly

Warm up

Will is thinking about what affects how strong a magnet is. His idea is that: 'long magnets are stronger than short ones'.

Which of these might also affect how strong a magnet is?

- The colour it is painted.
- How heavy it is.
- The surface it is on.
- The metal it is made from.
- Its shape.
- The direction it points.

Lift off

Will has come up with a way of testing his idea. However, his plan is in the wrong order.

A Add paperclips one by one.

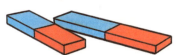

B Then do the test on each of the other magnets in turn.

C Keep on adding the paperclips until no more can be added.

D Record how many paperclips could be added to each magnet.

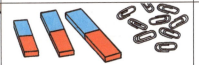

E Get some paperclips and some magnets of different sizes.

F Take the smallest magnet. Hold it upright.

Redraw his plan in order.

The booster

Will's plan is not yet complete. Some details are missing.

1. How could Will make sure his test was fair?
2. How many measurements should he take?
3. How should he record his measurements?
4. Now write out his complete plan in the best order.

Checkpoint

There are some other ideas you could test. Write down some other things that might make magnets stronger.

For example, you could test the idea that: 'horseshoe magnets are stronger than bar magnets'.

Comparing magnets

Bar charts help you to compare two sets of results

Warm up

Will did his test using 2cm, 3cm, 4cm, 5cm and 6cm long magnets. They were made out of the same metal and were the same shape.

Will made some predictions about what his test would find out. Which predictions seem sensible?

- Strong magnets will pick up fewer paperclips than weaker ones.
- Strong magnets will pick up more paperclips than weaker ones.
- The longer the magnet, the more paperclips it will pick up.
- Longer magnets are stronger than shorter ones and will pick up more paperclips.
- Magnets of the same length and shape can have different strengths.

Lift off

Will did his test and found out how many paperclips each magnet picked up. Here are his results in a bar chart. Study it carefully.

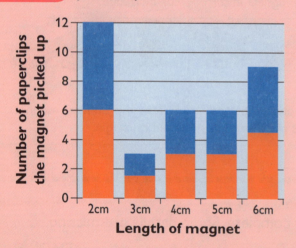

1. Which magnet picked up the most paperclips?
2. Which magnet picked up the fewest paperclips?
3. How many paperclips did the shortest magnet pick up?
4. How many paperclips did the longest magnet pick up?
5. Which two magnets picked up the same number of paperclips?

The booster

Compare Will's results with his predictions.

1. Do the results fit any of his predictions?
2. How would you explain Will's results?

Checkpoint

Try this test for yourself with your own magnets. Is there a pattern to your results?

Light wordpower

Some words help to describe ideas well

Warm up

If you want to talk and write about light, you need to know some key words. Find the 'light' words in this word snake.

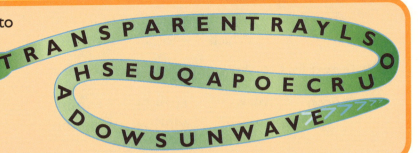

Lift off

Now let's make your 'Warm up' list longer and see what each word means.

1 Work with a friend and add some more words to your list.

2 Use the words to make a one-page glossary, just like the one at the back of this book.

A glossary is a list of words and their meanings.

The booster

Chloe has been thinking about light. Some of her ideas are not quite right, however.

Opaque materials make light shadows. Transparent materials make dark shadows.

b Sundials work because the size of a shadow gets bigger during the day.

a The Sun moves across the sky in one direction one day, and then moves back the next day.

c The Sun rises in the North and sets in the South because the Sun moves around the Earth.

Rewrite each thought so that it is correct, explaining why. One has been done for you.

*Opaque materials make **dark** shadows because no light can get through them. Transparent materials make **light** shadows because a bit of light can get through them.*

Checkpoint

This diagram shows how the Sun appears to move during the day.

Let's see if you can draw diagrams to show how:
a opaque materials make a shadow
b a sundial works
c the Sun rises and sets each day.

Shadows

When an object blocks light, a shadow is formed

Warm up

There are many sources of light. Which objects give out their own light? Which do not?

Write two lists to show you know the difference.

> torch   mirror   candle   moon   sun   lamppost
> firework   window   spoon   television

Gives out own light	Doesn't give out own light
torch	

Lift off

Shadows are formed when light from a source is blocked.

Rewrite these sentences in order so they tell you how a shadow is formed.

4 **A** Some light goes from the torch onto Teddy and it goes no further.

5 **B** Some light travels either side of Teddy onto the floor. This makes this area light.

2 **C** Teddy has blocked some of the light.

1 **D** Jack is shining his torch at his teddy.

3 **E** Behind Teddy there is dark shape where no light shines. This dark shape is the shadow.

The booster

Shadows are dark. They lack any detail of the object that forms the shadow. Draw the shadows of these three objects.

a    b    c

Checkpoint

Let's see if you can make some shadows of your own.

First, tape a piece of white paper on the wall. Stand in front of it. Ask your friend to shine the torch at you. A second friend can trace around your shadow. Swap with your friends so you each have a turn.

The Sun's shadows

The Sun appears to move across the sky

Warm up — Change the following times in the 12-hour clock to the 24-hour clock.

7 a.m.   9 a.m.   midday   2 p.m.   6 p.m.   midnight

Remember, to turn afternoon times into the 24-hour clock, you just add 12. That means 3 p.m. is 3 + 12 = 15:00.

Lift off — The Sun appears to move across the sky in a regular way.

| 07:00 | 09:00 | 11:00 | 12:00 | 13:00 | 15:00 | 17:00 |

1 At what time was the Sun highest in the sky?
2 Redraw the diagram adding in the position of the Sun at 9 a.m. and 1 p.m.
3 At what approximate time would sunrise and sunset be?

The booster — The Sun does not really move across the sky. Its apparent movement is caused by the Earth spinning on its axis.

This model shows the Earth (the globe) moving while the Sun (the torch) stays still.

Imagine what you would see if you stood on the globe and looked at the torch. The torch would appear to move even though you are standing still.

In the same way, the Sun appears to move as the Earth spins on its axis.

1 Draw a series of diagrams to show the globe moving steadily around.
2 Draw similar diagrams to show the Earth spinning while the Sun keeps still.

Checkpoint — Find out what time the Sun rises and sets in your town or village today.

Daytime shadows

Shadows change during the day

Warm up Imagine you are standing outside on a sunny day. Draw two diagrams to show how your body blocks light from the Sun to form:

a a short shadow at midday   b a longer shadow later in the afternoon.

Lift off The Sun forms different shadows as it appears to move across the sky.

1 Where is the Sun in the sky when it makes a short shadow?
2 Where is the Sun in the sky when it makes a long shadow?
3 Explain how the shape of your shadow changes during the day.

The booster The higher the Sun appears in the sky, the shorter the shadow. Chloe stuck a shadow stick in the ground and drew the shadow formed at different times in the day.

2p.m.   12 noon   7a.m.   5p.m.

1 Match each of these shadows to the correct time of day.
2 Draw the shadow you would expect to see at 10a.m.

Checkpoint The Sun has been used to tell the time for many years. Now you know how shadows change during the day, try this. Explain to your friend how a sundial works.

Predicting ⭐⭐

Tests need to be fairly done

Warm up

Chloe has learned a lot about how shadows are formed. She wondered what would happen if she used different materials to make some shadows.

Bubble wrap

Wood

Glass

Metal foil

Clingfilm

Greaseproof paper

Write down what else Chloe would need to make her shadows.

Lift off

Some materials stop light. Some let light though. The materials Chloe chose varied in how much light they let through.

Make a table like the one below. Put the materials Chloe chose for her test into the correct column.

Opaque materials let no light through.
Translucent materials let a little light through.
Transparent materials let a lot of light through.

Opaque materials	Translucent materials	Transparent materials

The booster

Chloe wondered if there would be any differences in the shadows made by the different materials. She knew the shapes would be different, but what else might be?

What do you think will happen when Chloe makes her shadows with the materials?

Checkpoint

Chloe now has all the information she needs to write her plan.

Write a complete plan for Chloe's test.

Are the predictions any good? ★★

Friction can be dangerous to you

Warm up

Chloe came up with several predictions.

- Opaque materials will form light shadows.
- Translucent materials form lighter shadows than opaque materials.
- Transparent materials will not form any shadows at all.

1. Which of these predictions do you think the test might show to be true?
2. Think of one more prediction that the test might prove.

Lift off

Here are Chloe's results. Look closely at the colour of the shadows.

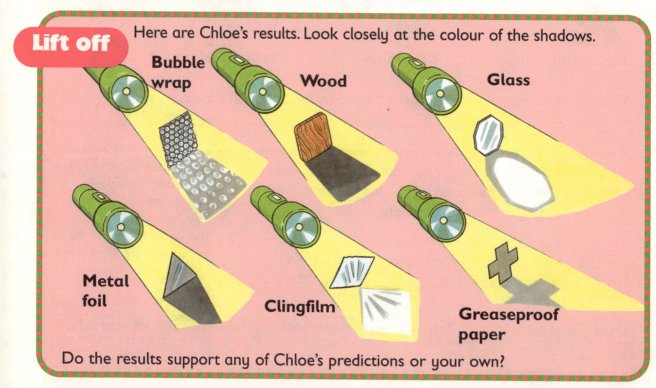

Bubble wrap, **Wood**, **Glass**, **Metal foil**, **Clingfilm**, **Greaseproof paper**

Do the results support any of Chloe's predictions or your own?

The booster

You can use your knowledge of science to help explain what happened in the test. For example, 'The transparent materials (glass and clingfilm) make a very faint shadow because they only block a little light and you can see the edges.'

Write a sentence with 'because' in it to explain why Chloe's correct predication was true.

Checkpoint

If Chloe were to rewrite her three predictions, what would she write now that she has the evidence of her tests?

Glossary

Axis
An imaginary line about which the Earth spins.

Bones
The parts of an animal's body that makes up its skeleton.

Canine
A pointed tooth used for holding and tearing food.

Decay
The rotting of a tooth caused by bacteria and sugars making acids.

Fair test
A scientific test in which some things are kept the same and one thing is changed.

Fruit
An edible, fleshy part of a plant that contains one or more seeds.

Germination
When a seed starts to grow and forms a small root and a shoot.

Humus
The part of the soil made from small pieces of dead plants and animals.

Incisor
A sharp tooth used for biting food.

Leaf
Green part of a plant that makes food for the plant.

Light
A kind of energy that makes things visible.

Magnet
A bar of metal which attracts some other metals to it.

Milk teeth
Your first set of teeth.

Molar
A tooth with a flat top used for grinding food.

Non-magnetic
A material that is not attracted to a magnet.

Opaque
A material that is opaque does not let any light through it.

Petal
The part of a plant that is usually brightly coloured.

Prediction
What you think might happen in a fair test.

Property
A characteristic of a material.

Roots
The part of a plant which holds it in the soil and takes up nutrients.

Sand
Small, rounded particles of rock, originally made from sandstone.

Seedling
A baby plant.

Shadow
A dark patch of shade formed when an object blocks out light.

Soil
A material in the upper layer of the Earth's surface formed mainly from ground-up rocks.

Stem
The main body or stalk of a plant.

Sundial
An instrument that tells the time using the Sun's shadows.

Sunrise
The time of day when the Sun first lights up the Earth.

Sunset
The time of day when the Sun disappears over the horizon.

Tooth
One of the hard, bone-like structures found in the mouth that is used for biting and chewing food.

Vegetable
A plant that has parts that are used for food, e.g. pea, cauliflower, onion.

Published by Letts Educational
The Chiswick Centre
414 Chiswick High Road
London W4 5TF
Telephone: 020 8996 3333
Fax: 020 8742 8390
E-mail: mail@lettsed.co.uk
Website: www.letts-education.com

Letts Educational is part of the Granada Learning Group.
Granada Learning is a division of Granada plc.

© Alan Jarvis and William Merrick 2003

First published 2003

ISBN 184085 9326

The authors assert the moral right to be identified as the authors of this work.

All rights reserved. No part of this publication may be reproduced, stored in a retrieval system, or transmitted, in any form or by any means electronic, mechanical, photocopying, recording or otherwise, without the prior permission of the Publisher or a licence permitting restricted copying in the United Kingdom issued by the Copyright Licensing Agency Ltd, 90 Tottenham Court Road, London W1P 9HE. This book is sold subject to the condition that it shall not by way of trade or otherwise be lent, hired out or otherwise circulated without the publisher's prior consent.

British Library Cataloguing in Publication Data
A catalogue record for this book is available from the British Library.

This book was designed and produced for Letts Educational by Ken Vail Graphic Design, Cambridge

Commissioned by Kate Newport

Project management by Phillipa Allum

Editing by Nancy Candlin

Illustrations by Graham-Cameron Illustration (Pat Murray)

Production by PDQ

Printed and bound in the Italy by Amilcare Pizzi